· REDISCOVERING RA~~~~

HAMPSHIRE

The north of the county

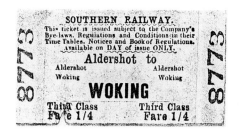

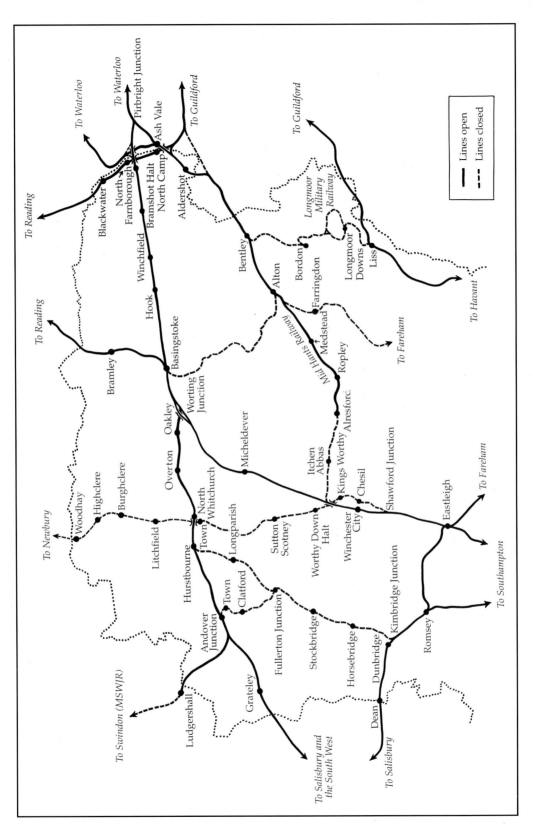

Map of the railways of north Hampshire, showing the principal locations and others illustrated in the book. The railways of Romsey, Eastleigh and Liss southwards are included in the companion volume dealing with the south of the county.

· REDISCOVERING RAILWAYS ·

HAMPSHIRE

The north of the county

A pictorial record of the area's railways past and present

Terry Gough

· RAILWAY HERITAGE ·

from

The NOSTALGIA Collection

First published in 2001

British Library Cataloguing in Publication Data

A catalogue record for this book is available from the British Library.

ISBN 1 85895 167 4

Past & Present Publishing Ltd
The Trundle
Ringstead Road
Great Addington
Kettering
Northants NN14 4BW

Tel/Fax: 01536 330588
email: sales@nostalgiacollection.com
Website: www.nostalgiacollection.com

Some of the material in this book first appeared in *British Railways Past and Present, No 21 Berkshire and Hampshire*, by the same author and published by Past & Present Publishing Ltd in 1994.

All tickets and other items of ephemera are from the author's collection.

Map drawn by Christina Siviter

Printed and bound in Great Britain

Past and Present

A Past & Present book
from
The NOSTALGIA Collection

CONTENTS

ANDOVER JUNCTION: The down milk empties pass through Andover Junction on 2 September 1962, hauled by 'Merchant Navy' Class No 35014 *Nederland Line.* **The bay for the Romsey line is behind the train.**

  By the time of a visit on 7 May 1986, Andover had lost many of its features. The Romsey line had closed, and the semaphore signals, the signal box, the centre running line and some of the sidings had been removed. A DMU of Class 3H (now 205), No 1402, forms the 15.55 from Reading to Portsmouth Harbour, hardly a direct route and involving a reversal at Salisbury. *Both TG*

WORTING JUNCTION was a favourite location, with good views of the diverging lines. In the foreground is the down Bournemouth line, while on the bridge is the up Bournemouth, under which pass the West of England lines. On 12 April 1962 the down 'Atlantic Coast Express' is worked by 'Merchant Navy' Class No 35024 *East Asiatic Company*.

A reminder of past times was witnessed almost exactly 33 years later when preserved 'King Arthur' Class No 30777 *Sir Lamiel* took a special train from Waterloo to Salisbury. *Both TG*

INTRODUCTION

This is the second of two volumes on the railways of Hampshire, showing changes over the past few decades. Although I have used the majority of photographs from an earlier edition, covering the county in more detail has enabled me to introduce a significant amount of new material, both past and present.

The former London & South Western Railway (LSWR) main line from Waterloo passes through Hampshire, dividing just beyond Basingstoke for Weymouth and the West of England. Other railway companies also reached Hampshire: the Great Western Railway (GWR) from Reading to Basingstoke, and the South Eastern & Chatham Railway (SECR) from Kent to Reading along the Blackwater Valley. There were also two much smaller companies, the Midland & South Western Junction Railway (MSWJR) from Cheltenham to Andover Junction, and the Didcot, Newbury & Southampton Railway (DNSR), which passed under the LSWR at Whitchurch. Following the privatisation of British Rail (BR), the situation has come full circle. The major railway company in north Hampshire is South West Trains, but other companies, including Wales & West, Thames Trains, Anglia Railways and Virgin Trains, run services to the county from other parts of the country.

The LSWR had several secondary routes and branch lines. The Andover Junction to Romsey line was surprisingly under-utilised, but were it still open today it could play a significant role, such has been the increase in demand for both leisure and business travel across the county.

Motive power has always been varied in north Hampshire, with steam, diesel and electric trains common even in the 1950s. Electrification reached parts of the county in the 1930s, and the first diesel multiple units (DMUs) in 1957. Hampshire was to be host to the last main-line steam operation in the country. Electrification now covers much of north Hampshire, although the West of England line beyond Worting Junction remains in the hands of DMUs.

Changes will no doubt continue to take place, both in the types of rolling-stock and the pattern of services. What is common today may well have become a rarity in a few years' time.

Terry Gough
Sherborne, Dorset

ACKNOWLEDGEMENTS

I thank BR for the provision of a lineside pass and the private individuals, companies and military authorities who gave permission for me to enter their properties. I am grateful to Colin Pattle and Dick Ware for the provision of information on present-day operations, and I also thank those photographers who willingly provided material to fill the gaps in my own photographic coverage. As always, I thank my wife Cynthia for her support.

BIBLIOGRAPHY

The Basingstoke & Alton Light Railway, Edward C. Griffiths (1947)
The Bordon Light Railway, Peter A. Harding (1987)
The London & Southampton Railway Guide (James Wyld, 1839)
The Longparish Branch Line, Peter A. Harding (1992)
The Midland & South Western Junction Railway, T. B. Sands (Oakwood Press, 1979)
Passengers No More, G. Daniels and L. Dench (Oakwood Press)
The Railways of Southern England, Vols I, II and III, Edwin Course (Batsford, 1973/74/76)
The Reading to Tonbridge Line, R. W. Kidner (Oakwood Press, 1978)
The Southern Railway Collection: Branch Lines Recalled, Terry Gough (Silver Link Publishing, 1999)
  Hampshire and Dorset, Terry Gough (Silver Link Publishing, 2000)
  Surrey and Berkshire, Terry Gough (Silver Link Publishing 1999)
The Waterloo-Southampton Line, R. W. Kidner (Oakwood Press, 1983)

SOUTH WESTERN MAIN LINE
Farnborough to Shawford Junction

FARNBOROUGH (1): The boundary with Surrey is a short distance east of Farnborough on the LSWR main line. On 22 August 1964 'West Country' Class No 34014 *Budleigh Salterton* heads toward Waterloo on the 8.49am from Salisbury.

The same location is still readily accessible and a visit on 28 April 1995 saw several interesting workings, including two Class 20s on a weedkilling train. The leading locomotive is No 20904 *Janis*, while at the rear is No 20901 *Nancy*. *Both TG*

London and South Western Ry.

787

TO

Farnboro'

FARNBOROUGH (2): On 16 May 1964 'Battle of Britain' Class No 34052 *Lord Dowding* stops at the station with the 2.54pm Waterloo to Salisbury service. The line through Farnborough to Basingstoke was not electrified until 1967 and, apart from a very few diesel-worked trains during the transition period, all trains were steam-operated.

It is now normally only the semi-fast electric trains that stop at Farnborough (now called Farnborough Main). However, during the International Air Show all express trains stop here. On 12 September 1992 Class 47 No 47707 *Holyrood* leaves on the 09.50 Waterloo to Exeter St David's train. On the up side Class 423 No 3046 works a semi-fast Basingstoke to Waterloo train. *Both TG*

FARNBOROUGH (3): A good view of the station could be had from the sidings at the west end. On 15 October 1960 'Schools' Class No 30904 *Lancing* leaves the station on the 12.39pm Waterloo to Basingstoke train.

An unusual working was captured on 3 September 1992 when electro-diesels of Classes 71 and 73 took a passenger train towards Bournemouth. The Class 71 carries its original number of E5001.

Another surprise occurred on 2 May 1995 when a special train to test central door-locking mechanisms passed through Farnborough, as seen in the third photograph. The front unit is No 316997, formerly of Class 307 No 307118. This was four-coach overhead-electric stock, converted in 1960 from DC to high-voltage AC operation and latterly allocated to Neville Hill, Leeds. *All TG*

BRAMSHOT HALT was closed in 1946, but the site was easily recognisable almost 20 years later as 'Merchant Navy' Class No 35005 *Canadian Pacific* ambled past on the 2.54pm semi-fast Waterloo to Basingstoke train on 27 June 1964 – something of an insult to such a powerful locomotive!

The platforms have been removed and a huge ugly pipe has been built over the railway, necessitating a high vantage point to obtain a clear view. A visit was made on 26 March 1994 to record what was advertised as the last working on the Exeter line of Class 50 locomotives. Nos 50050 and 50007 *Sir Edward Elgar* head west on a special passenger train as a 'Wessex Electric', constituting the 07.45 Poole to Waterloo train, passes in the other direction. *Both TG*

REDISCOVERING RAILWAY

WINCHFIELD (1): Standard Class '4MT' No 76034 enters the station on the 2.47pm Salisbury to Waterloo train. The first two coaches are non-corridor stock, built at Eastleigh by BR and not ideal for long distances; passengers would have been far more comfortable in the Bulleid coaches at the rear of the train.

On 24 September 1988 a Class 47 passes through Winchfield with a 'vans' train – a new meaning for the term! *Both TG*

WINCHFIELD (2): A Nine Elms to Southampton Docks freight train passes through Winchfield in July 1965 hauled by Class 'N' No 31842. The centre platforms had been abandoned many years previously and there is evident decay in the goods yard, despite it still being in use.

REDISCOVERING RAILWAYS

The 1993 view shows that both the centre platforms and goods yard have finally gone, together with the signal box and imposing gantry. This was the last year of locomotive-hauled passenger trains to Salisbury and Exeter, but until delivery of the entire fleet of 'South Western Turbos' (Class 159) all manner of odd motive power was used. On 22 May 1993 the 13.35 Waterloo to Yeovil Junction is formed of DMUs Nos 207001 and 207013 of Class 207. *Both TG*

HOOK: Looking west from the road overbridge gives an excellent view of the railway. 'West Country' Class No 34021 *Dartmoor* approaches at speed in August 1965.

Apart from track simplification and electrification, little has changed in the 1993 view. On 22 May a 'Networker' unit of Class 465, No 465237, approaches the station under test, prior to allocation to services in Kent. *Both TG*

BASINGSTOKE (1): A Waterloo to Bournemouth express approaches Basingstoke behind 'West Country' Class No 34009 *Lyme Regis* on 12 September 1964. To the left are the carriage sidings, while the extensive freight yards were at the country end of the station. The signals were pneumatically operated throughout their existence and were not replaced with 'colour lights' until electrification of the line.

On 26 September 1987 a special working leaves the carriage sidings behind Class 37 No 37116. Class 37s were very unusual on the South Western main line until the spring of 1993 when several were introduced for use on freight trains in the area. *Both TG*

London and South Western Railway.

TO

787)

Basingstoke.

BASINGSTOKE (2): In this view of the station from the London end on 12 April 1962, the 8.46am Salisbury to Waterloo train stands on the up local line behind 'King Arthur' Class No 30451 *Sir Lamorak*. In the far platform a rebuilt 'West Country' waits to take its train to Reading.

Although the view is now partially blocked, a comparison is still possible. On 20 July 1998 Class 159 No 159004 forms the 09.32 Yeovil Junction to Waterloo service. *Both TG*

65

BASINGSTOKE (3): Following the closure of the Somerset & Dorset line, the 'Pines Express' was routed via Basingstoke and Reading, and is seen at the former bound for Manchester on 1 August 1964. The locomotive is 'Merchant Navy' Class No 35005 *Canadian Pacific*.

There are now many more workings from the South of England to the North, and even in winter there is a bi-hourly service through Basingstoke. On 17 March 1994 an 'InterCity 125' waits for a door to be closed before heading for Edinburgh as the 11.20 from Bournemouth. *Neil Davenport/TG*

BASINGSTOKE (4): Class 'S15s' were freight engines, but were sometimes seen in charge of secondary passenger trains. No 30509 enters Basingstoke on empty stock that will form the 3.12pm to Woking. On the right is the engine shed.

On 15 October 1998 the author had just put his camera away as the sun had all but set, when from the west appeared the unmistakable shape of a 'Heritage' DMU. Fortunately it was moving very slowly, allowing time for the camera to be retrieved. The front and rear coaches are ex-unit No L842 of Class 101. The centre coach, named *Iris*, is Derby Laboratory coach No 19 (ex DB975010), built in 1957 as a single-car unit with driving compartments at both ends. *Both TG*

BASINGSTOKE (5): At the same end of the station, a freight train for Southampton Docks passes through on the down local line on 12 April 1962 behind Class 'S15' No 30510. The rear of the motive power depot is on the left.

On 26 September 1987 Class 205 DMU No 205030 crosses from the down main to the local line after working a train from Reading. On the right is the all-stations train to Bournemouth formed of a Class 423 electric multiple unit (EMU), while on the left are locomotives of Classes 73 (No 73118) and 33 (No 33027). *Both TG*

BASINGSTOKE MPD housed an interesting range of motive power on 2 September 1962, ranging from LSWR to BR steam locomotives and a diesel shunter. In the foreground are Classes '4MT' No 75077 and 'S15' No 30514. The shed was also regularly host to 'foreign' engines of GWR origin, and on 12 September 1964 the LNER was represented by No 4472 *Flying Scotsman*.

The MPD was closed in 1967 and demolition is witnessed two years later in the third photograph. The site is now occupied by light industrial units and offices. *All TG*

WORTING JUNCTION (1) is seen looking toward Basingstoke. A down heavy freight train for the West of England, hauled by Class 'S15' No 30498, waits for a passenger train to pass on the fast line. The up fast line is occupied by a Bournemouth to Waterloo train headed by a 'West Country' Class 'Pacific'.

The location is now far less cluttered with no signals or telegraph poles. On 28 May 1988 a down freightliner heads for Southampton behind a Class 47. This could have been taken a decade later, the only difference being the locomotive livery. *Both TG*

WORTING JUNCTION (2): An up vans train hauled by 'King Arthur' Class No 30782 *Sir Brian* is descending from Battledown Flyover on 12 April 1962.

On 28 May 1988 Class 50 No 50008 *Thunderer* passes with the 06.42 Exeter St David's to Waterloo service. All locomotive-hauled trains on this line were replaced by DMUs in 1993. *Both TG*

WORTING JUNCTION (3): After steam ended, many of the trains from Waterloo were push-pull operated using Class 33 diesels, although some, such as this one, seen on 18 October 1986, were conventionally hauled. The engine is No 33106 and the train is the 15.10 Waterloo to Exeter St David's.

A sleeper on the Southern! InterCity introduced a sleeper between Scotland and Dorset in the summer of 1988, but it only survived until the end of the winter 1991/92 timetable. By definition sleepers are difficult to photograph during daylight hours, but a Class 47 and its train were caught in the early morning light in May 1992, on the penultimate run of this service. The train had left Glasgow and Edinburgh the previous evening and was due to arrive in Poole at 08.18. *Both TG*

WORTING JUNCTION (4): A light load for 'Merchant Navy' Class No 35005 *Canadian Pacific*, on the 8.37am Bournemouth West to Waterloo slow train on 6 September 1964.

The odd combination of a diesel locomotive and an electric unit was photographed on 18 October 1986. The former is push-pull-fitted Class 33 No 33114 and the multiple unit is No 004, formerly the motor coaches from 4 SUB No 4361, now a de-icer. *Both TG*

MICHELDEVER (1) is the first station south of Worting Junction o the Bournemouth line, and serves the nearby village and, mo importantly for the railway, the adjacent oil storage depot. Th extensive sidings were used to store railway stock awaiting repai at Eastleigh or for scrap. The 'past' photograph was taken from th remains of the centre island platform that served the up and dow fast lines; by this time only local trains, using the platforms on th far left and right, stopped at Micheldever. On 12 August 196 'Merchant Navy' Class No 35021 *New Zealand Line* works th 3.30pm Waterloo to Bournemout train.

Major changes have taken place Micheldever. The island platform were re-instated in 1966 and there now only one up and one down lin The old down local platform ha been demolished and the up loc platform is no longer used excep for access to the centre platforms v a subway. Two Class 37s take Freightliner to Southampton on 2 April 1993. *Both TG*

REDISCOVERING RAILWAY

MICHELDEVER (2): All manner of interesting and unusual stock was stored at Micheldever in the summer of 1965 4 SUB EMU No 4305 dwarfs London Underground stock, to the left of which are several SR horse-boxes.
Following clearance of old stock, the sidings were re-opened for regular oil trains, and one is being shunted in the yard on 1 July 1989 by Class 47 No 47318. By the mid-1990s the depot was closed to rail traffic, but the sidings are still in place. *Both TG*

WINCHESTER CITY (1): When the first DMUs were introduced in Hampshire in 1957, they ran only between Southampton and Winchester City, and here we see new two-coach unit No 1109 arriving as the 12.25pm from Southampton Terminus on 8 October 1957. A third coach was added to these units in 1959 and they later became designated Class 205.

All long-distance trains were steam-operated, and on 26 August 1961 'Lord Nelson' Class No 30860 *Lord Hawke* takes the 8.12am from Bournemouth West to Waterloo.

Winchester station has been refurbished and still represents an excellent example of a main-line LSWR station. On 18 April 2001 the 10.00 Brighton to Reading train is worked by a member of the newly introduced Class 170, No 170302. At the time of writing these units were also under test between Basingstoke and Salisbury, with a view to using them in conjunction with Class 159s on the West of England line from the summer of 2001. *All TG*

WINCHESTER CITY (2): The yard was on a very tight curve adjacent to the station, necessitating the use of short-wheelbase engines, normally Class 'B4', one of which was allocated to the tiny shed seen in the background of the top picture opposite. No 30096 is on duty in August 1961.

The yard has since been taken up and the various small buildings in the foreground removed, but the Pickfords building has been converted into offices. *Both TG*

WINCHESTER CITY (3): On 6 May 1987 Class 204 No 204004 forms the 16.55 from Reading to Portsmouth Harbour, while on 11 July 1998, photographed further along the platform, a Virgin Cross Country train hauled by Class 43 No 43198 leaves Winchester as the 05.30 Manchester to Bournemouth service. *Both TG*

SHAWFORD JUNCTION: Winchester also had a station at Chesil on the former Didcot, Newbury & Southampton Railway (DNSR) (see pages 68-69) and this met the LSWR at Shawford Junction. The down 'Bournemouth Belle', hauled by 'Merchant Navy' Class No 35014 *Nederland Line*, passes a special train hauled by Class '3MT' No 82029 on the DNSR line on 6 September 1964.

The DNSR has been closed for many years, although the platelayers' hut has survived. The main line has become almost completely obscured, and the new bridge (just visible in the distance on the left) is part of a new road system associated with the controversial extension of the M3 motorway across Twyford Down. This was under construction at the time of the 'present' photograph, 18 October 1992, and further major roadworks have subsequently made the location inaccessible. *Both TG*

WEST OF ENGLAND MAIN LINE

Worting Junction to Grateley

OAKLEY: Several of the intermediate stations between Basingstoke and Exeter were closed during the 1960s, Oakley being one of them. Here we see the station in 1968, by this time privately owned.

Although some of the closed stations have since been re-opened, Oakley remains closed. The main building is used as offices and the former goods yard is occupied by a builder's merchant. Class 159 No 159007, introduced a few days previously, speeds through as the 11.50 Gillingham to Waterloo service on 22 May 1993. *Both TG*

OVERTON was the next station, serving the adjacent banknote-paper factory, as well as the nearby village. Seen here in 1967, little has changed since the day it was built.

A visit on 21 May 1993 found that the station had been completely rebuilt and the platforms lengthened in preparation for the introduction of the 'South Western Turbo' trains. The 19.51 Basingstoke to Salisbury train is formed of Class 207 No 207001. *Both TG*

WHITCHURCH NORTH (1) consisted of one down platform and an island up platform, the north face being used as the terminating point for trains from Fullerton Junction until closure of that line in 1931 (see page 45). It was renamed plain Whitchurch following closure of the former DNSR station nearer the town (see page 64). Class '5MT' No 73088 leaves on the 7.20am Waterloo to Salisbury train in August 1964.

Several changes are evident in the spring of 1993. The station buildings on both platforms have been renovated, the main building on the down side is almost obscured by new buildings in the old yard, and the up platform is no longer an island. Both platforms have been extended westward, thus giving the impression that the two photographs are taken from different points. Class 159 No 159010 enters Whitchurch forming the 18.35 Waterloo to Exeter St David's service. *Both TG*

REDISCOVERING RAILWAYS

WHITCHURCH NORTH (2): On 12 August 1989 Class 50 No 50017 works the 05.56 from Exeter St David's to Waterloo, including a 4TC trailer set normally used for push-pull working with Class 33s.

These trains are now in the hands of Class 159 and also Class 170 DMUs from Summer 2001. This is No 159021 forming the 07.42 Gillingham to Waterloo service on 28 August 1998. *Both TG*

ANDOVER JUNCTION (1): There were two small engine sheds side by side at Andover Junction, one belonging to the LSWR and the other to the Midland & South Western Junction Railway (MSWJR), both of which passed into BR ownership. The site of the former now contains little-used sidings and the latter is occupied by a warehouse. On 14 May 1955 Class 'U' No 31619 shunts in front of the shed area. A similar event was recorded on 3 March 1998 when Class 37 No 37211 arrived to collect some grain wagons (see page 41). *J. H. Aston/TG*

REDISCOVERING RAILWAYS

ANDOVER JUNCTION (2): Push-pull-fitted Class 33 No 33115 propels the 09.38 Exeter St David's to Waterloo service into Andover Junction on 31 January 1987. The present-day equivalent is far more comfortable and faster; on 3 March 1998 Class 159 No 159014 arrives at Andover as the 09.32 Yeovil Junction to Waterloo service. *Both TG*

ANDOVER JUNCTION (3) was the meeting point of lines from Eastleigh, Southampton and the former MSWJR from Swindon and beyond; there was a bay for the Eastleigh and Southampton trains at the London end of the station on the down side. The two engine sheds occupied the site of the white-roofed factory in the background.

Andover formally lost its junction status in 1964, although the Swindon line is still open for MOD traffic as far as Ludgershall. An amazing sight greeted the uninformed when preserved 'King Arthur' Class No 777 *Sir Lamiel* pulled out of Andover on a westbound special train on the morning of 18 October 1992. *Both TG*

ANDOVER JUNCTION (4): A Salisbury to Waterloo train approaches Andover on the last day of January 1987. The stock consists of push-pull trailer coaches of set No 410 (Class 4TC) being propelled by a Class 33 diesel.

Today's monopoly held by DMUs is rarely broken, although there is an occasional locomotive-hauled train in the form of freight for the Ludgershall MOD branch. In the spring of 1998 a train was introduced on an experimental basis to take grain to Scotland. Wagons were attached to the regular slurry train from Quidhampton, diverted via Andover for the purpose. It is seen here arriving behind Class 37 No 37073 *Fort William/An Gearasdan* on 3 March. *Both TG*

GRATELEY is the last station on the Exeter main line in Hampshire, and was once a busy interchange for the branch services to Bulford military camp. The station had clearly seen better days and closure looked imminent when the 'past' photograph was taken in 1965.

In fact, Grateley is still open and is served by Salisbury trains, several of which continue to Exeter. The station has been refurbished since this 13 June 1987 photograph was taken and is enjoying an upsurge in passenger traffic. Class 50 No 50002 *Superb* passes through the station on the 13.10 Waterloo to Exeter train. *Both TG*

ANDOVER TO ROMSEY LINE

ANDOVER TOWN was a scruffy station, even before boarding up and removal of the track. It is seen here in 1966.

Road development makes location of the site today very difficult. Part of the railway towards Andover Junction has been used for a new road and in the vicinity of the station a roundabout has been built. This is the 'present' view; it shows no clues that it is the correct location, but behind the hedge on the right is the remains of the Romsey-bound platform, including part of the wooden waiting shelter. *Both TG*

London and South Western Ry.
787
TO
ANDOVER TOWN

London and South Western Ry.
— 787
FROM WATERLOO TO
CLATFORD

CLATFORD saw the occasion
special train, in addition to norm
service trains. On 6 September 19
Class '3MT' No 82029 pauses at th
station on its way to Andover
mark the closure of the line.

All trace of the station has bee
removed and bungalows built o
the site. The clues to the location a
the house in the background an
the trackbed. *Both TG*

FULLERTON JUNCTION: Nowhere was more decrepit on this line (and indeed on the whole of the SR) than Fullerton Junction. Although this photograph was taken about a year after closure, the front section of canopy on the Romsey-bound platform had been in this state for decades. From here another line ran north-east to the West of England main line at Hurstbourne. Despite grand plans, it was nothing more than a country branch line and lost its passenger service in 1931, though part was retained for freight until 1956.

The station buildings were surely early candidates for demolition, but surprisingly some have been used as part of what are now private houses. This is the same location (from a higher angle) in 1992. *Both TG*

Above An early dark blue LSWR luggage label for Fullerton Bridge. The name was changed to Fullerton in 1871 and later to Fullerton Junction.

Left Another special train on the Andover to Romsey line, standing at Fullerton Junction. The locomotive is Class 'Q' No 30548 and the train will continue to Andover and Salisbury. *TG*

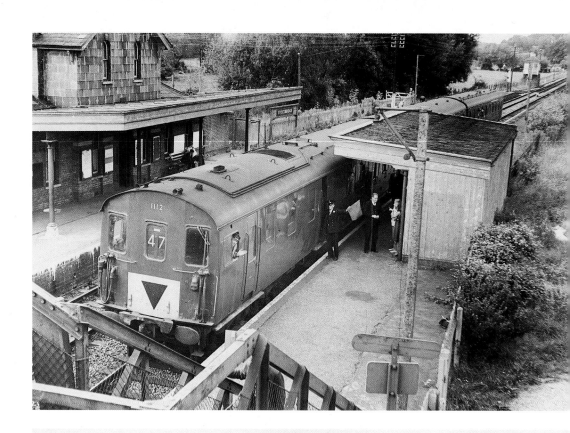

TOCKBRIDGE: 'Right away' for an Andover to Portsmouth train in the spring of 1964. The line had become run own and most buildings had not been painted or repaired for many years.

The second photograph, taken from the other end of the station, shows the signal box and an Andover-bound train. he unit is Class 3H No 1130 on the last day of services in September 1964. In the third view final waves are being ade as a special passes by on the last day, providing a further example of how run down the line had become, with e remains of a once busy goods yard in the foreground.

Today there is no trace of the station, or indeed the railway, in the Stockbridge area. All has disappeared under a ad improvement scheme, which involved construction of a roundabout and road on the station site. This is a ightly more distant view, but in the same direction as the 'past' photographs. *All TG*

Opposite HORSEBRIDGE (1): A visit to the station several months after closure found it still intact, if a little overgrown. The whole line remained in this state for many months before finally being dismantled during 1968 and 1969.

Horsebridge station was later sold and the new owners have retained much of the railway atmosphere. An LSWR-designed corridor coach stands in the platform and a signal box and signals have been added. Although not of LSWR origin, they contribute greatly to the scene. *Both TG*

This page HORSEBRIDGE (2): I have visited the station on many occasions, and these three photographs show the view from the Andover end when the line was open, during dismantling and at the present day. The river bridge remains and forms part of a footpath; the road bridge in the background, while still in existence, is more difficult to see as the cutting has been filled in. *All TG*

MOTTISFONT: 'Hampshire' DMU No 1130 works the 11.30am Andover Junction to Portsmouth service; even on this, the last day of passenger services, little interest was shown in the railway, as can be seen by the absence of either passengers or bystanders on the platforms.

A visit on 18 October 1992 found the station building in use as a private house and a garden laid out where once was the track and platforms. *Both TG*

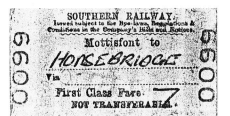

Left The last SR First Class Mottisfont blank ticket in stock, issued on the last day of services.

KIMBRIDGE JUNCTION: The Andover line met the line from Salisbury at Kimbridge Junction, 3¼ miles north of Romsey. A special train hauled by Class '3MT' No 82029 is seen coming off the Andover line on the last day of services, 6 September 1964.

At the site of the junction on 18 October 1992 the 13.10 Portsmouth Harbour to Cardiff service is formed of Class 158 No 158823. Although very much overgrown in the intervening years, the course of the line to Andover is still evident in many places. The farm buildings seen in the 'past' photograph still stand, hidden from view by the trees. *Both TG*

London and South Western Ry.
787
From WATERLOO TO
DUNBRIDGE

DUNBRIDGE (1) was an attractive country station in good repair, in contrast to those on the Andover line; this is the view looking towards Salisbury in 1968.

The signal box, traditional crossing gates and signals have all been replaced, and the view on 9 March 1999 shows Class 158 No 158815 on the 07.30 Cardiff Central to Portsmouth Harbour service. *Both TG*

DUNBRIDGE (2): 'Hampshire' DMU (Class 205) No 205029 stops briefly at Dunbridge forming the 09.40 service from Salisbury to Portsmouth & Southsea on 13 June 1987.

Dunbridge was renamed 'Mottisfont (Dunbridge)' from May 1988, but it has since reverted to plain Dunbridge. The present-day service is very sparse with 3-hour gaps on weekdays. Class 156 No 156462 stops on a morning train to Bristol Temple Meads. *All TG*

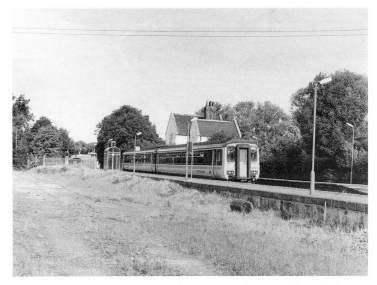

DEAN station is just in Hampshire, with the county boundary passing over the railway immediately to the west of the level crossing. In this July 1978 view the signal box, which is in Wiltshire, still existed. A recent view shows a train straddling the boundary as the leading unit, No 155311 of Class 155, enters the station. *Both TG*

LINES TO READING

FARNBOROUGH NORTH (1): BR Class '4MT' No 76032 is seen entering Farnborough North with a set of narrow-bodied coaches forming the 5.05pm Reading to Guildford service on 11 April 1964.

Through trains from the North of England to Brighton are occasionally routed this way rather than via Kensington Olympia, while trains from the North to Poole are normally routed via Basingstoke. One such train, diverted because of engineering works, is the 08.50 from Liverpool to Poole on 4 April 1993, hauled by a member of Class 47. *Both TG*

FARNBOROUGH NORTH (2): An evening train, the 4.20pm from Reading to Redhill, calls at Farnborough North on 26 March 1964 behind Class 'N' No 31869. On 15 October 1992 Cross Country unit No L594 of Class 119 stops at the station, now devoid of its signal box; the train is the 15.10 Reading to Redhill. *Both TG*

BLACKWATER in SR days was a rather drab station. In later years, particularly in the 1970s, it suffered from extensive vandalism, so it was a pleasant surprise to find the station very well kept in a spring 1999 visit. The original buildings have gone and the A30 road bridge in the background has been widened. Class 158 No 158748, on hire to Virgin Trains, forms the 11.35 Liverpool Lime Street to Portsmouth Harbour service. *Lens of Sutton/TG*

BRAMLEY: There are two stations on the former GWR Basingstoke to Reading line, one of which is in Hampshire. This is Bramley, looking toward Reading in 1966, at the time under the auspices of the Southern Region.

The original buildings have been retained, but modernisation has eliminated the signal box and traditional level crossing gates. On 15 October 1998 Class 165 No 165134 forms an afternoon Thames Trains service from Reading to Basingstoke. There is a half-hourly service for much of the day, augmented by trains run by South West Trains and Virgin Trains. *C. L. Caddy/TG*

BRAMLEY MILITARY RAILWAY: Just south of Bramley station was a large goods yard for the nearby military establishment, which had its own railway. Seen on the Bramley Military Railway in 1971 is a Ruston Hornsby 0-6-0 diesel locomotive with an SR brake-van and former London Underground coaches.

The military depot was closed in 1987 and its railway abandoned. There is little evidence in this photograph to show where the railway once ran, although much of the track in the goods yard, which is to the right and out of sight, was still in place at the time of this visit in 1993. There were proposals to use the site as a transport museum, but these have been abandoned and the site is currently derelict. *Both TG*

THE DIDCOT, NEWBURY & SOUTHAMPTON LINE

WOODHAY was the first station on the DNSR south of Newbury, and is seen here on 12 December 1959 looking towards Newbury. The passenger service was withdrawn three months later. The DNSR line was of strategic importance during both World Wars; in 1942 it was doubled from Newbury to Woodhay, and passing loops at other stations were lengthened.

The line south of Newbury closed completely on the last day of 1962, and the site of Woodhay station is now abandoned; although the platforms are still in place, the embankment and bridge at the north end of the station have been removed. *Chris Gammell/TG*

HIGHCLERE was typical of the stations on this line, with an attractive main building and small goods yard, as can be seen in this February 1960 view, looking south. There was, however, potential for confusion as the nearest village was Burghclere, rather than Highclere. The station is today in private ownership and stands in extensive and most attractive grounds. *Chris Gammell/TG*

BURGHCLERE itself is seen here, looking towards Newbury in February 1958. A Southampton train has just departed, from which only one passenger has disembarked. The station served the hamlet of Old Burghclere and the timetable noted that this was the alighting point for Kingsclere.

The old goods yard behind the camera is still in use by a coal merchant and the station building was under renovation at the time of this March 1993 visit. *Chris Gammell/TG*

LITCHFIELD looks forlorn in this 12 December 1959 view, having already lost the Newbury-bound line even before closure. The signal box in the background was built during the Second World War to assist in coping with the large number of additional freight trains between the Midlands and Southampton Docks. Similar ugly signal boxes were built at some of the other stations.

The A34 trunk road parallels the railway from just south of Burghclere almost to Winchester, and this has resulted in the removal of the embankment in some places. It has also made the task of identifying some locations difficult and Litchfield is an example. The station now finds itself almost buried behind earthworks resulting from construction of the upgraded A34, which is in a cutting immediately to the left of the camera. *Chris Gammell/TG*

WHITCHURCH TOWN was also photographed in December 1959. Another lightly patronised station, a sole passenger leaves with his own local means of transport. The LSWR main-line station of Whitchurch (by this time called Whitchurch North) was about 1¼ miles away.

This is yet another DNSR station that has survived into the 1990s as a private house. A public footpath runs parallel to what was the trackbed, while the A34 road, which used to pass through the town to the east of the line, now runs to the west of the old station. *Chris Gammell/TG*

SUTTON SCOTNEY was at the intersection of the A34 and A30 trunk roads and the station was situated just to the south of this point. Here it is, again in December 1959, with a Southampton-bound train attracting a little revenue from the local post office.

The buildings have gone and an office block has been erected on the site, but part of the platforms are still in existence and the yard is used by Associated Asphalt Ltd. The road overbridge is just visible behind the wooden fencing, and the house to the left still stands. *Chris Gammell/TG*

WORTHY DOWN HALT was a bleak and uninspiring place at which to alight, particularly in winter. It is referred to on the 1-inch Ordnance Survey Map as 'Worthy Down Platform', which shows it almost at the end of a road apparently leading to nowhere. In fact the road led to a military establishment, hence the need for the halt, which was opened in 1918. The photograph again dates from December 1959.

In 1993 the old platform is still to be found amongst the trees, and the trackbed is used as a footpath. The entrance to the halt from the nearby road overbridge still exists, although overgrown. *Chris Gammell/TG*

INGS WORTHY was another decrepit station, still open when
is photograph was taken. It was built in 1909, 18 years after the
ne itself was opened.

The station has been completely obliterated and the site is now
nder the A34 road; a visit on summer Saturdays is not
commended as the constant stream of cars precludes photography
d is also dangerous! The site of the goods yard seen in the right
stance of the 'past' photograph is where the roofs of the modern
uildings are located in front of the row of houses. *Chris Gammell/TG*

WINCHESTER CHESIL occupied a cramped location immediately beyond a tunnel under St Giles Hill on the eastern side of the city; the tunnel portal is just visible beyond the train, and the station fitted between this and the footbridge. The line then continued south by skirting the city and meeting the LSWR Bournemouth main line at Shawford Junction (see page 33 and Silver Link's *The Southern Railway Collection: Hampshire and Dorset*). Class 'E1' No 31067 leaves Chesil on a special train from London Bridge to Eastleigh via Newbury on 22 May 1960. Between 1958 and 1961 a DMU service was run on summer Saturdays between Southampton and Winchester Chesil to relieve pressure at Winchester City station. Winchester Chesil to Shawford Junction was closed completely in April 1966.

By 3 April 1993 the trackbed has become a road and the station site is occupied by a multi-storey car park. The footbridge is still in use, although it has been rebuilt. *Both TG*

ALDERSHOT (1): The Alton line leaves the West of England main line at Pirbright Junction in Surrey, and the first station in Hampshire is Aldershot. There were regular local freight workings in the area and, after one such trip on 15 October 1960, Class '700' No 30350 of Guildford Shed is turned. Although the turntable and signal box have gone, the location is easy to identify from the country end of Aldershot station. *Both TG*

ALDERSHOT (2): This photograph of the goods yard captures a scene unchanged for decades, with ex-LSWR Class '700' No 30325 shunting on 9 June 1962.

Rationalisation from the late 1960s has dramatically changed the scene. The goods yard has gone and even the bus depot, which belonged to the Aldershot & District Traction Company, is almost deserted. Miraculously there is still freight on the line in the form of a nightly oil train. On Saturdays this runs during daylight hours and on 31 October 1992 was hauled by Class 37 No 37220 *Westerleigh*. *Both TG*

BENTLEY was the junction for the Bordon branch, which was closed to passengers in September 1957. Three years later a special train was run consisting of a push-pull unit of pre-Grouping coaches and Class 'M7' No 30028. This is the view from the up side looking toward Aldershot.

Bentley is still open for passengers and is served by Waterloo to Alton trains. The line west has been singled and the tracks through the station are signalled for reversible working. Class 423 No 3405 works 'wrong line' through the station in the late afternoon of 9 March 1993. *Both TG*

REDISCOVERING RAILWAY

BORDON was almost 5 miles south of Bentley, and its railway served the surrounding military towns and was the interchange point for the northern terminus of the Longmoor Military Railway (LMR), which had a station adjacent to the LSWR station. Here Class 'Q1' No 33035 leaves Bordon on a special train on 14 March 1964.

Today the station area is occupied by industrial units. The only items to link the two photographs are the trees in the background and the fact that the approach road to the estate is named Station Road. Other clues, out of sight, are a row of Victorian houses and some more obvious remains of the LMR terminus. *Hugh Ballantyne/TG*

NO 2 RANGE HALT, LMR: The LMR saw occasional special through trains from BR, such as this train near No 2 Range Halt on 30 April 1966. The engine, Army Department No AD600 *Gordon*, worked the train through from BR down the Portsmouth main line earlier in the day. The engine went to the Severn Valley Railway after closure of the LMR.

The land once occupied by the railway is still owned by the Ministry of Defence and is used for training purposes, as can be seen on 9 March 1993. *Both TG*

LONGMOOR DOWNS (1) was the main station on the LMR, and the railway's headquarters. A special train leaves the station in 1966 for a trip round the Hollywater Loop behind Army Department No 196. Following closure this engine was moved to the Mid Hants Railway. The LMR trackbed is now used for the testing of military vehicles. *Both TG*

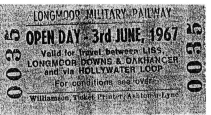

LONGMOOR DOWNS (2): This is the station in 1967, with two W
0-6-0 tank engines on duty. The site is now part of a new section
the A3 London to Portsmouth trunk road, uncharacteristically qu
early one winter morning in 1996. The only reminder of the railw
is the water tower, which can be glimpsed between the trees on t
far left. The shape of the trees in the background also confirms t
location. *Both TG*

REDISCOVERING RAILWAY

ALTON (1) was the end of the electrified line from Waterloo, and beyond here were steam-operated services to Southampton and Fareham. There was also a line to Basingstoke, which closed in 1936. In this 1967 view a Class 73 electro-diesel locomotive shunts in the yard.

In later years the Southampton service was usually operated by 'Hampshire' DMUs, as seen in the second photograph. This is unit No 1121, which was later disbanded and the coaches used in reformed units.

Significant changes for the better have taken place at Alton, which still has a frequent electric service to London. Electric trains can now use either of the platforms in view, a crossover has been added and there is still a freight service. The oil train seen here on 10 March 1993, being worked by Class 60 No 60024 *Elizabeth Fry*, runs from Eastleigh via Woking, where it reverses; on arrival at Alton it reverses again in order to gain access to the nearby Holybourne Oil Terminal. The journey time is approximately 2½ hours; were the line to Winchester still open, the journey could be accomplished in three-quarters of an hour. Alton is also the eastern terminus of the Mid Hants Railway, whose trains use the outer face of the island platform on the right. *All TG*

ALTON (2) is seen on 8 October 1957, as Class 'M7' No 30028 waits with the 12.05pm train for Eastleigh for the
connecting service from Waterloo; the following month the service was taken over by DMUs. The Waterloo service
are currently worked by EMUs; early BR slam-door units are being replaced by modern units of Class 458. Despi
delivery a year earlier, on 3 April 2001 only two were in passenger use. This is No 458014 leaving Alton on the 11.3
to Waterloo. *Both TG*

LTON (3): This is the far platform in BR days prior to the re-opening of the line westward toward Alresford. This platform is currently used by Mid Hants Railway trains, which use larger engines and more modern rolling-stock than BR did when the line was steam-operated. *Both TG*

REDISCOVERING RAILWAYS

ALTON (4): Newly built 'Hampshire' DMU No 1111 approaches Alton forming the 9.53am service from Southampton Terminus on 6 August 1958.

The second photograph offers a glimpse of the past on 15 October 1960 when Class 'M7' No 30028 worked a special push-pull train out of Alton to Farringdon on the Meon Valley line.

Subsequently, re-instatement of services on part of the Mid Hants line has resulted in the regular appearance of steam at Alton, such as this train approaching the station in March 1993. *All TG*

REDISCOVERING RAILWAY

MEDSTEAD & FOUR MARKS (1): The first photograph is a study of Class '700' No 30325 at Medstead & Four Marks with a freight train from Eastleigh on 18 April 1956. A few weeks later, on 2 June, motor set No 36, forming the 7.42am from Eastleigh to Alton, stands at this pleasant station, which is within easy walking distance of Four Marks, situated by the main road between Guildford and Winchester.

Double-headed steam trains were seen on this line when main-line trains were diverted due to engineering works, and the occasional special train also came this way, for example on 3 April 1966 when Classes 'U' No 31639 and 'Q1' No 33006 worked a railway enthusiasts' train. Today steam is the norm, and the new order at Medstead & Four Marks is a Class 'N', approaching the station with a train bound for Alton. *TG/J. H. Aston/TG/TG*

MEDSTEAD & FOUR MARKS (2): On 9 May 1956 the 12.05pm from Alton is hauled by Class 'M7' No 30125. This first view contrasts with the abandoned look on 3 April 1966 shortly before closure. In the intervening period the oil lamps have been replaced by electric light, using the same lamp-posts.

It is debatable whether the station will ever regain its use for commuters, as the main road has been upgraded making it easy to drive to Alton for stations to London. Today's preserved station has deliberately gone back in time with the re-introduction of some 'oil' lamps; it is beautifully maintained and further enhanced on 22 May 1993 by the arrival of a train hauled by 'West Country' Class No 34105 *Swanage. J. H. Aston, TG (2)*

Mid-Hants Railway
3rd Class
**MEDSTEAD &
FOUR MARKS
to ALRESFORD
and RETURN**

HALF FARE
as advertised
VALID DAY OF ISSUE

Issued subject to
the Conditions of
Winchester and
Alton Railway PLC

1

N⁰ 0883

ROPLEY (1), a quiet country station, is seen first on 21 September 1963. Although well kept, it has obviously seen better days, as the up platform has long since been taken out.

Dramatic changes have since taken place, and Ropley is busier than it has ever been, with a new up platform and double track through the station. An engine shed has been built on the site of the goods yard, giving a tantalising view of both steam and diesel locomotives, and the SR electric lamps have been replaced by LSWR-style 'oil' lamps. *Both TG*

ROPLEY is seen again on 2 June 1956, with Class '700' No 30350 running in gently with the 8.26am Eastleigh to Alton freight train.

The area to the left has since been transformed and is occupied by an engine shed, as seen on 25 July 1987. In the shed yard are Classes 'S15' No 506, 'West Country' No 34016, 'T9' No 30120 and '4MT' No 76017. *J. H. Aston/TG*

ALRESFORD (1): In the last few years of BR ownership, Alton to Winchester services were operated by 'Hampshire' DMUs, now Class 205. Nos 1108 and 1121 pass at Alresford on the last day of BR services.

Alresford is now the administrative headquarters of the Mid Hants Railway. Diesels are still used on some trains, in this instance Class 25 No D5217 on the last train of the day in October 1992. *Both TG*

British Transport Commission (S)
ALRESFORD
PLATFORM TICKET 1d.
Available ONE HOUR on DAY of ISSUE ONLY
NOT VALID IN TRAINS NOT TRANSFERABLE
To be given up when leaving Platform
FOR CONDITIONS SEE OVER

ALRESFORD (2): Two further glimpses of the past at Alresford. Class 'M7' No 30379 propels the 10.16am Eastleigh to Alton train on 2 June 1956, while a special visited the line at the beginning of 1966, using No 30837 as motive power. This was the 'S15 Commemorative Railtour' and the train is waiting for a clear road before heading for Winchester. *J. H. Aston/TG*

ITCHEN ABBAS (1) was the next station towards Winchester, and in the month prior to closure DMU No 1130 calls for non-existent passengers.

All hope of re-opening the line at Itchen Abbas and beyond has been extinguished, as the station site has been used for a small housing development. Two of the houses are appropriately named 'The Down Side' and 'Beeching'. *Both TG*

ITCHEN ABBAS (2): Another view of the 'S15 Commemorative Railtour' in 1966 near Itchen Abbas. Much of the line in this area has been obliterated and the 'present' view is typical of all that is left. *Both TG*

REDISCOVERING RAILWAY

GAZETTEER OF NORTH HAMPSHIRE'S RAILWAYS

Mileages are taken (where applicable) from the Southern Railway Standard Timetables dated 30 September 1935. Stations were opened and closed on the same dates as their respective lines unless otherwise stated.

Farnborough-Shawford Junction (LSWR)

Stations: Farnborough (33¼m from Waterloo), Bramshot Halt (35¾m), Fleet (36½m), Winchfield (40m), Hook (42½m), Basingstoke (48m), Worting Junction (no station; 51½m), Micheldever (58¼m), Winchester (66¾m), Shawford Junction (no station; 69m).

Farnborough was renamed Farnborough (Main) about 1980. Fleet was Fleetpond until 1.7.1869. No record has been located regarding the change of name of Shapley Heath to Winchfield; it is referred to as Winchfield, Hartley Row or Hook in a guide to the LSWR dated 1839. Micheldever was called Andover Road until 2.1856, although it was also referred to as Popham. Winchester was called Winchester City between 26.9.1949 and 10.7.1967.

Opening and closure: Woking to Shapley Heath (Winchfield) opened 24.9.1838, Shapley Heath to Basingstoke 10.6.1839, and Basingstoke to Winchester 11.5.1840. Winchester opened 10.6.1839 when the line was opened to Southampton. Bramshot Halt opened 10.5.1913, Fleet in 1847 and Hook 2.7.1883. The line was electrified in 1967 with partial services as far as Basingstoke 2.1.1967, to Winchester and Southampton 3.4.67, and full services from 10.7.67. The line and all stations are still open, except Bramshot Halt, closed 6.5.1946.

Route and traffic: The main line enters Hampshire gently rising in a long and attractive cutting just before Farnborough. It is virtually straight all the way to Basingstoke. After a level stretch between Farnborough and Fleet, it rises gradually most of the way to Worting Junction. From Basingstoke the line begins to turn toward the south, and after Micheldever again runs in a straight line to Winchester; it falls most of the way, passing through tunnels just north of Micheldever and again north of Winchester.

The line is very busy with a frequent service of passenger trains, both expresses and all-stations trains, most of which are to and from Waterloo. There are some freight trains along the eastern part of the line, but many more on the southern end, travelling mostly between the Southampton area and Reading (and beyond). This section also sees regular trains from other parts of the country.

Worting Junction-Grateley (LSWR)

Stations: Oakley (52½m from Waterloo), Overton (55¾m), Whitchurch (59¼m), Hurstbourne (61¼m), Andover Junction (66½m), Grateley (72¾m).

Whitchurch was called Whitchurch North from 26.9.1949 to 2.10.1972. Andover Junction was plain Andover until 6.3.1865 and again from 1964.

Opening and closure: Basingstoke to Andover opened 3.7.1854, and Andover to Grateley and Salisbury 1.5.1857. Oakley closed 17.6.1963. Hurstbourne opened 1.12.1882 and closed

6.4.1964. The branch from Grateley to Newton Tony in Wiltshire opened 1.10.1901, closed to passengers 1920 and completely 30.6.52. Battledown Flyover at Worting Junction opened 30.5.1897 to carry the up Southampton line over the West of England line.

Route and traffic: At Worting the West of England line passes under Battledown Flyover, which carries the up line from Southampton. Between Oakley and Hurstbourne the line falls gradually and thereafter rises and falls in quick succession with a maximum of 1 in 165 through Grateley. The view from the train becomes increasingly attractive after Worting Junction and this is maintained for the rest of the journey right through to Exeter.

The line has traditionally been well used both by passenger and freight trains. During the summer period there was a succession of long passenger trains heading for the holiday resorts of Devon and Cornwall. There was also a reasonable loading of local traffic. The 1960s saw the very rapid decline of the line, and the complete loss of freight traffic, from which it has never recovered. However, passenger services have in recent years been improved and many trains are full all year round. Further developments are under consideration.

Andover-Romsey (LSWR)

Stations: Andover Town (¾m from Andover Junction), Clatford (2¾m), Fullerton (5½m), Stockbridge (8½m), Horsebridge (11¾m), Mottisfont (14¼m), Kimbridge Junction (no station; 14¾m).

Fullerton was Fullerton Bridge until 10.1871, then Fullerton until 5.1889 and Fullerton Junction until 7.1929.

Opening and closure: Andover Junction to Romsey (and Redbridge) opened 6.3.1865; closed as far as Kimbridge Junction 7.9.1964.

Route and traffic: This line passed along the attractive Test Valley, but the few places it served did not in latter years generate sufficient business to ensure survival. The only intermediate town was Stockbridge, the other stations serving much smaller communities. The line did, however, provide a link between Andover and the Southampton area and it is surprising that this was not better used. It left Andover on a sharp curve and thereafter followed the River Anton until joining the River Test at Fullerton, which it followed to Romsey.

Longparish branch (LSWR)

Stations: Wherwell (1¼m from Fullerton), Longparish (3¼m), Hurstbourne (7½m).

Longparish was Long Parish until 1.7.1890.

Opening and closure: Fullerton to Longparish and Hurstbourne opened 1.6.1885. Wherwell and Longparish closed 6.7.1931, but the line was retained as far as Longparish for freight until 28.5.1956.

Route and traffic: This little-used line followed the River Test from Fullerton to Longparish, then took a more northerly route to join the West of England main line near Hurstbourne.

Andover Junction-Swindon (MSWJR)

Station: Weyhill (3½m) is the only station in Hampshire on the MSWJR line.

Opening and closure: Andover to Grafton in Wiltshire opened 1.5.1882. The line closed to passengers 11.9.1961 and to general freight 24.3.1969, but is still open to Ludgershall for military traffic.

Route and traffic: Despite the grand title of the railway company, this line declined in importance during the early BR period and became little more than a local route. In its heyday long-distance passenger trains ran between Andover and Cheltenham, with through coaches to other destinations, but this was not sustained. By the early BR period there was only one through train per day. There was also general freight and military traffic, and the line was heavily used by the latter during both World Wars. The southern remnant of the line through Weyhill to Ludgershall is still in use and serves the military establishments on Salisbury Plain.

Romsey-Salisbury (LSWR)

Stations: Kimbridge Junction (no station; 3¼m from Romsey), Dunbridge (3¾m), Dean (7¾m

Dunbridge was called Mottisfont (Dunbridge) between 16.5.1988 and 29.5.1994.

Opening: Bishopstoke (Eastleigh) to Salisbury opened to freight 27.1.1847 and to passengers 1.3.1847.

Route and traffic: This line serves as a valuable link between Southampton and the South Coast, and Bristol and South Wales. It has always enjoyed a good service of both passenger and freight trains. A frequent passenger service is still provided, although most trains are non-stop between Romsey and Salisbury. There are also a few freight trains. After leaving the Test Valley at Kimbridge Junction the line heads west with the River Dun, and over the county boundary at Dean.

Farnborough North-Reading (SECR)

Stations: Farnborough North (10¼m from Guildford) and Blackwater (12¾m) are the only stations in Hampshire on the Reading line. Those south of Farnborough are in Surrey, north of Blackwater in Berkshire. Farnborough North was Farnborough until 9.7.1923.

Opening and closure: Farnborough to Reading opened 4.7.1849, and Farnborough to Ash 20.8.1849. The line and listed stations are still open.

Route and traffic: This is a very useful line linking Guildford and the South with Reading, the Midlands and the North, without the necessity of going through London. In Hampshire it passes along the Blackwater Valley, no longer a particularly attractive journey as much has been given over to industrial development and new roads. Local and long-distance passenger traffic is heavy and there are frequent trains between Gatwick Airport and Reading. There have always been through trains from other parts of the country and this tradition continues, albeit on a much smaller scale. The line has always been busy with military personnel and freight, although the latter has now ceased.

Basingstoke-Reading (GWR)

Station: Bramley (5m from Basingstoke) is the only station in Hampshire on the GWR line, the other stations to Reading being in Berkshire.

Opening and closure: Reading (Southcote Junction) to Basingstoke (GWR station) opened 1.11.1848. Basingstoke (GWR) station closed 1.1.1932 and all trains thereafter used the LSWR station.

Route and traffic: This is another very useful south-north link, with frequent long-distance passenger and freight trains that continue to this day. There is also a local service between Basingstoke and Reading. On leaving Basingstoke the line turns north through rather uninspiring countryside. Just before Bramley it passes the now closed Bramley Military Railway. It passes into Berkshire between Bramley and Mortimer.

Didcot, Newbury & Southampton line (DNSR)

Stations: Woodhay (3¼m from Newbury), Highclere (5½m), Burghclere (7½m), Litchfield (10m), Whitchurch Town (13¾m), Sutton Scotney (19½m), Worthy Down Halt (22¼m), Kings Worthy (24½m), Winchester Chesil (26¼), Shawford Junction (no station; 28½m).

Opening and closure: Newbury to Winchester Cheesehill (later Chesil) opened 4.5.1885, and Winchester Cheesehill to Shawford 4.9.1891. A spur from Worthy Down Halt to the main line at Winchester Junction opened 5.5.1943 and closed 1951. Newbury (Enborne Junction) to Winchester Chesil closed 7.3.1960. Winchester Chesil re-opened from 18.6.1960 to 10.9.1960 and from 17.6.1961 to 9.9.1961 for passenger trains via Shawford Junction; it closed completely 4.4.1966.

Route and traffic: This is another line with a grand title, and whose fortunes were similar to the MSWJR. It wound through a lightly populated part of the county at a leisurely pace, the only towns ever likely to provide much revenue being Newbury and Winchester. The line climbed almost all the way from Enborne Junction to just beyond Burghclere, much of which was at 1 in 106. It then descended at the same gradient to Whitchurch and continued to drop, more gently, to Sutton Scotney. There was a sharp climb toward Worthy Down, and thereafter a fall all the way to Winchester, again mostly at 1 in 106. The approach to Winchester was through a tunnel. Beyond Winchester, the line included a brick-built viaduct on the approach to Shawford Junction.

The line was strategically significant during the war years, as it offered a route between the Midlands and Southampton Docks without going too close to London. Additional track and signalling was installed to cope with extra traffic, but once peace was restored usage fell dramatically. There was, however, a reasonable flow of freight traffic, and it is regrettable that the line has not survived. Winchester Chesil was re-opened for a short while for local passenger trains from Southampton, in the early days of the 'Hampshire' DMUs, as on summer Saturdays Winchester City would become too congested. The view from the train was attractive but not breathtaking.

Aldershot-Winchester (LSWR)

Stations: Aldershot (35¼m from Waterloo via Ash Vale), Farnham (in Surrey; 38¼m), Bentley (42m), Alton (47m), Medstead & Four Marks (51¼m), Ropley (54½m), Alresford (57m), Itchen Abbas (60¾m), Winchester Junction (no station; 63¾m), Winchester (66m).

Opening and closure: Pirbright Junction to Farnham opened 2.5.1870 and Aldershot Junction South to Aldershot Town 1.5.1879. Farnham to Alton opened 28.7.1852. Alton was resited in 1865. Woking to Farnham was electrified 3.1.1937 and a full service between Woking and Alton began 4.7.1937. Alton to Winchester Junction opened 2.10.1865. Medstead & Four Marks opened 8.1868 as Medstead; the name was changed 1.10.1937. Alton to Winchester Junction closed 5.2.1973. Alresford to Alton re-opened in stages as the Mid Hants Railway: Ropley to Alresford 30.4.1977, Ropley to Medstead 28.5.1983, and Medstead to Alton 25.5.85.

Route and traffic: After traversing the built-up area around Aldershot, the line passes into Surrey until 1¾m before Bentley, whence it follows the River Wey to Alton through pleasant countryside. Beyond Alton it is a very hilly route, beginning with a long climb at 1 in 60 to the summit at Medstead & Four Marks. Beyond here the line is undulating, but not excessively steep. The line traverses high embankments and deep cuttings, but the landscape changes by Alresford as it approaches the Itchen Valley, which it used through to Winchester Junction, as does the main line south from this point. Some parts of the trackbed of the abandoned line west of Alresford have been built over.

East of Alton passenger and freight traffic was mainly local, with the addition of main-line trains between Waterloo and Southampton when the main line was blocked, and the situation has little changed, except that there are no longer any main-line trains. The only local freight is of oil at Holybourne, 2 miles before Alton. The Alton-Winchester line was also rural in nature (apart from the above-mentioned through trains), most trains starting or terminating at Alton. Alresford was the only intermediate station to serve a town, the others being for surrounding villages. There was growth at Four Marks, but not sufficient to prevent closure.

Bordon branch (LSWR)

Stations: Kingsley Halt (2¾m from Bentley), Bordon (4¾m).

Opening and closure: Opened 11.12.1905, closed to passengers 16.9.1957, and completely 4.4.1966. Despite this official closure, special passenger trains ran until 30.4.1966. Kingsley Halt opened 7.3.1906.

Route and traffic: A shuttle service was provided between Bentley and Bordon, and there were also occasional military trains. General freight traffic was light, again augmented by military traffic. The line passed through pleasant countryside along the edge of Alice Holt Forest. It climbed from Bentley at a maximum of 1 in 156, but soon began to descend much of the way to Kingsley Halt. There were no significant gradients until just before Bordon, when there was a short climb at 1 in 105.

Longmoor Military Railway

Stations: Oakhanger (¾m from Bordon), Whitehill (2¼), No 2 Range Halt (3m), Woolmer (3½), Longmoor Downs (4½m).

Opening and closure: Opened in 1906. Bordon closed 1966 and the remainder of the line 31.10.1969.

Route and traffic: The LMR station at Bordon was adjacent to the LSWR station, while other stations served various camps and ranges. The headquarters was at Longmoor Downs, where there was a locomotive depot and works. The railway was built mainly for training purposes, but a passenger service, restricted to military personnel, was also provided. A loop line running from a junction at Whitehill to Longmoor Downs was added in 1942. This gave the facility for continuous running to simulate various operating conditions.

Alton-Fareham (LSWR)

Station: Farringdon (50½m from Waterloo) is the only station in north Hampshire on the Fareham line (see *Rediscovering Railways: Hampshire, the South of the County*).

Farringdon was called Faringdon Platform between 1.5.1932 and 8.7.1934.

Opening and closure: Opened 1.6.1903. Farringdon opened 1.5.1931. Closed beyond Farringdon 7.2.1955, the section as far as Farringdon being retained for freight until 3.8.1968.

Route and traffic: The line diverged from the Winchester line at Butts Junction and was engineered to be double-track throughout, but was only laid as single track beyond the junction. From 1935 the up line between Alton and the site of Butts Junction was used only by Winchester trains, and the down line by Fareham trains.

Alton-Basingstoke (LSWR)

Stations: Bentworth & Lasham (5m from Alton), Herriard (7¾m), Cliddesden (11¼m), Basingstoke (14¼m).

Opening and closure: Opened 1.6.1901, closed 1.1.1917, re-opened 18.8.1924 and closed again 12.9.1932, except from Basingstoke to Bentworth & Lasham for general freight and from Alton to Treloar's Hospital, where there was a private station called Alton Park. Basingstoke to Bentworth & Lasham section closed completely 30.5.1936, except for ½m at the Basingstoke end that served a factory; this closed 1967. The Treloar's Hospital section closed officially 31.7.1967.

Route and traffic: This is yet another line that traversed a sparsely populated area between two large towns, resulting in little intermediate traffic. There was the potential for farm traffic, but the railway never took advantage of this. Heading north from Butts Junction, there were no major engineering works on the line, although there were tight curves and steep gradients, with several at 1 in 50. The line climbed steadily as far as Lasham, then more steeply between Lasham and Herriard. Beyond Herriard the line descended most of the way (again at a maximum of 1 in 50) to the junction with the main line at Basingstoke.

INDEX OF LOCATIONS

Page number in **bold** refer to the photographs; other entries refer to the Gazetteer section.